THE FACES
OF JESUS

THE FACES

OF JESUS

A LIFE STORY

by Frederick Buechner

PARACLETE PRESS

BREWSTER, MASSACHUSETTS

2005 First and Second Printing

Copyright 1974, 2005 by Frederick Buechner

ISBN 1-55725-455-9

Library of Congress Cataloging-in-Publication Data
Buechner, Frederick, 1926-
The Faces of Jesus / by Frederick Buechner.
    p. cm.
Originally published: Croton-on-Hudson, N. Y.: Riverwood Publishers,
    1974.
ISDN 1–55725–455–9
1. Jesus Christ—Art. I. Title.
    N8050.B87 2005
    232—dc22
        2005005878

10 9 8 7 6 5 4 3 2

Published by Paraclete Press
Brewster, Massachusetts
www.paracletepress.com

Printed in the United States of America

CONTENTS

INTRODUCTION

He had a face...

Whoever he was or was not, whoever he thought he was, whoever he has become in our memories since and will go on becoming for as long as we remember him—exalted, sentimentalized, debunked, made and remade to the measure of each generation's desire, dread, indifference—he was a man once, whatever else he may have been. And he had a man's face, a human face.

Ecce homo, Pilate said—*Behold the man*—yet we tend to shrink back from trying and try instead to behold Shakespeare's face, or Helen of Troy's, because with them the chances are we could survive almost anything—Shakespeare's simper, say, or a cast in Helen's eye. But with Jesus the risk is too great; the risk that his face would be too much for us if not enough, either a face like any other face to see, pass by, forget, or a face so unlike any other that we would have no choice but to remember it always and follow or flee it to the end of our days and beyond. Like you and me he had a face his life gave shape to, and that shaped his life and the lives of others, and with part of ourselves I think we might turn away from the mystery of that face, that life, as much of the time we turn away from the mystery of life itself. With part of ourselves I think we might avoid meeting his eyes, if such a meeting were possible, the way at certain moments we avoid meeting our own eyes in mirrors because for better or worse they threaten to tell us more than we want to know. This is with part of ourselves. But there is another part, the dreaming part, the part that runs to meet in dreams truths that in the world itself we run from.

To say he had a face is to say that like the rest of us he had many faces as the writers of the Old Testament knew who used the Hebrew word almost exclusively in its plural form. To their way of thinking, the face of man is not a front for him to live his life behind but a frontier, the outermost, ever-changing edge of his life itself in all its richness and multiplicity, and hence they spoke not of the face of a man or of God but of his faces. The faces of Jesus then—all the ways he had of being and of being seen. The writers of the New Testament give no description of any of them because it was his life alive inside them that was the news they hawked rather than the color of his eyes. When you think the world is on fire, you don't take time out to do a thumbnail sketch. Nobody tells us what he looked like, yet of course the New Testament itself is what he looked like, and we read his face there in the faces of all the ones he touched or failed to touch: in the apostle Peter's face as he sat at dawn by the high priest's fire and heard the cock crow all the ghosts back to their rest except his own, or in the face of Judas leaning forward to plant his kiss in the moonlit garden; in the face of the leper, the wise man, the centurion, Mary's face. You glimpse the mark of his face in the faces of everyone who ever looked toward him or away from him, which means finally of course that you glimpse the mark of him also in your own face.

You turn toward his face in your face the way you might turn from shadows toward the light that cast them, or from the storm toward the eye of the storm where everything is still. The face of Jesus as light and stillness.

"He set his face to go to Jerusalem" the Gospels say, set it for a time which he does not have to be God to know is coming as he latches his feet under the soft belly of the ass he rides.

At the Last Supper he rises from the table to stand in silence, and if, like a rose, time has a center, a heart, his face is that center, and all our times pulse out from it like petals as he raises his life to his lips, his death.

At the end, he is dimly appalled at how little he understands of what is happening to him. Understands that the tongue he used to talk with is dry and thick as a stone. Understands that there are faces he once knew watching him, that there was a holy man in a river once, a woman somewhere who drew water from a well. Understands that there is a wine-soaked rag being held up to him as to a woman in labor and understands he also must labor now to thrust and anguish out into the howling world himself.

The apostle Paul writes: "God, who commanded the light to shine out of darkness, hath shined in our hearts to give the light of the knowledge of the glory of God in the face of Jesus Christ" (KJV), and to at least one part of that even unbelief can say amen: that it would take no less than God, if there were a God, to enable men to see God's glory in that shambles of a face.

Paul saw it, and for centuries all sorts and kinds of people have seen it—bright ones and stupid ones, good ones and bad ones, young ones and old ones—until little by little they come to look like what they dream toward. Paul saw that too, saw faith as transfiguration, as the faltering growth toward glory of even fools and rascals like himself.

This was the final mystery as he understood it, and at the farthest reach of his understanding he tried to set it down as such in black and white. What is the ultimate purpose of God in his creation? To make worlds, to make us, to make life in all its wildness and beauty? "[T]he whole creation groaneth and travaileth in pain together until now" (KJV), he says—for all we know, God himself groaneth and travaileth—until the last grim hold-out finally capitulates, is transformed "unto a perfect man, unto the measure of the stature of the fullness of Christ" (KJV). In other words, the ultimate purpose of God in his creation is to make Christs of us, Paul says.

Take it or leave it, the face of Jesus is, if nothing else, at least a face we would know anywhere—a face that belongs to us somehow, our age, our culture; a face we somehow belong to. Like the faces of the people we love, it has become so familiar that unless we take pains we hardly see it at all. Take pains. See it for what it is and, to see it whole, see it too for what it is just possible that it will become: the face of Jesus as the face of our own secret and innermost destiny:

The face of Jesus as our face.

1

ANNUNCIATION

"He had a face . . ."

"Before Abraham was," Jesus said, "I am." Who can say what he meant? Perhaps that just as his death was not the end of him, so his birth was not the beginning of him.

Whatever it is that history has come to see in him over the centuries, seen or unseen it was there from the start of history, he seems to be saying, and even before the start. Before Abraham was—before any king rose up in Israel or any prophet to bedevil him, before any patriarch or priest, temple or Torah—something of Jesus existed no less truly for having no name yet or face, something holy and hidden, something implicit as sound is implicit in silence, as the Fall of Rome is implicit in the first atom sent spinning through space at the creation. And more than that.

Jesus does not say that before Abraham was, he was, but before Abraham was, he *is*. No past, no future, but only the present, because only the present is real. Named or unnamed, known or unknown, there neither has been or ever will be real time without him. If he is the Savior of the world as his followers believe, there never has been nor ever will be a world without salvation.

But even for the timeless, to enter time is to divide it into before and after, then and now, just as to enter space is to divide it into here and there, me and you. Whatever the story of Jesus may be to the high angels, to us it must, like any other story, involve a beginning. The place where his story begins is a place. The time when it begins is a time. The person it begins with is a girl:

"And in the sixth month the angel Gabriel was sent from God unto a city of Galilee, named Nazareth, to a virgin espoused to a man whose name was Joseph, of the house of David; and the virgin's name was Mary.

"And the angel came in unto her, and said, 'Hail, thou that art highly favored, the Lord is with thee: blessed art thou among women.' And when she saw him, she was troubled at his saying, and cast in her mind what manner of salutation this should be.

"And the angel said unto her, 'Fear not, Mary: for thou hast found favor with God. And, behold, thou shalt conceive in thy womb, and bring forth a son, and shalt call his name JESUS. He shall be great, and shall be called the Son of the Highest: and the Lord God shall give unto him the throne of his father David: and he shall reign over the house of Jacob forever; and of his kingdom there shall be no end.'

"Then said Mary unto the angel, 'How shall this be, seeing I know not a man?'

"And the angel answered and said unto her, 'The Holy Ghost shall come upon thee, and the power of the Highest shall overshadow thee: therefore also that holy thing which shall be born of thee shall be called the Son of God. And, behold, thy cousin Elisabeth, she hath also conceived a son in her old age: and this is the sixth month with her, who was called barren. For, with God nothing shall be impossible.'

"And Mary said, 'Behold the handmaid of the Lord; be it unto me according to thy word.' And the angel departed from her." (KJV)

The angel says, "Don't be afraid, Mary."
He tells her not to be afraid because
the floor has failed her and the sheltering
wall no longer gives her shelter; not to be afraid
because most of what is familiar to her has faded
and flaked away like a painting. Heaven has flooded
in. And heaven kneels before her now with out-
stretched wings. But she is not to be afraid.

She is not to be afraid of all that lies beyond her: a lonely birth on a winter's night, a child she was never to understand and who never had time to give her much understanding, the death she was to witness more lonely and more terrible than the birth. "*Behold*," the angel says, "you will conceive in your womb and bear a son." Behold. He is telling her to open her eyes.

The Annunciation. As the ancient prophecies foretold, it is a virgin who is to bear the holy child. "The Holy Ghost shall come upon thee," the angel announces, "and the power of the Highest shall overshadow thee." It is not old Joseph but God who is the father. Paul, Mark, Matthew, the earliest writers about Jesus, say nothing of a virgin birth, but by the time Luke wrote his Gospel, it had come to seem that nothing less wonderful could account for the wonders he was gospeling. This extraordinary life could have had a beginning no less extraordinary. History creates heroes, but saints seem to arrive under their own steam. Evil evolves, but holiness happens.

Mary pondered these things in her heart, and countless generations have pondered them with her.

Mary's head is bowed, and she looks up at the angel through her lashes. There is possibly the faintest trace of a frown on her brow. "How shall this be, seeing that I know not a man?" she asks, and the angel, the whole Creation, even God himself, all hold their breath as they wait for what she will say next.

"Be it unto me according to thy word," she says, and jewels blossom like morning glories on the arch above them. Everything has turned to gold.

A golden angel. A golden girl. They are caught up together in a stately, golden dance. Their faces are grave. From a golden cloud between them and above, the Leader of the dance looks on.

The announcement has been made and heard. The world is with child.

2

NATIVITY

History creates heroes...
holiness happens

Some say that ever 'gainst that season comes
Wherein our Savior's birth is celebrated,
The bird of dawning singeth all night long;
And then, they say, no spirit dare stir abroad,
The nights are wholesome, then no planets strike,
No fairy takes, nor witch hath power to charm,

"So hallowed and so gracious is the time"—these lines from the first scene of Hamlet in a sense say it all. We tend to think of time as progression, as moment following moment, day following day, in relentless flow, the kind of time a clock or calendar measures. But we experience time also as depth, as having quality as well as quantity—a good time, a dangerous time, an auspicious time, a time we mark not by its duration but by its content.

On the dark battlements of Elsinore, Marcellus speaks to his companions of the time of Jesus' birth. It is a *hallowed* time he says, a holy time, a time in which life grows still like the surface of a river so that we can look down into it and see glimmering there in its depth something timeless, precious, other. And a *gracious* time, Marcellus says—a time that we cannot bring about as we can bring about a happy time or a sad time but time that comes upon us as grace, as a free and unbidden gift. Marcellus explains that Christmas is a time of such holiness that the cock crows the whole night through as though it is perpetually dawn, and thus for once, even the powers of darkness are powerless.

Horatio's answer is equally instructive. "So have I heard and do *in part* believe," he says to Marcellus, thus speaking, one feels, not just for himself but for Shakespeare and for us. In part believe it. At Christmas time it is hard even for the unbeliever not to believe in something, if not in everything. Peace on earth, good will to men; a dream of innocence that is good to hold onto even if it is only a dream; the mystery of being a child; the possibility of hope—not even the canned carols piped out over the shopping center parking plaza from Thanksgiving on can drown it out entirely.

For a moment or two, the darkness of disenchantment, cynicism, doubt, draw back at least a little, and all the usual worldly witcheries lose something of their power to charm. Maybe we cannot manage to believe the Christmas story with all our hearts. But as long as the moment lasts, we can at least believe that it is of all things the one most worth believing. And that may not be as far as it sounds from what belief is. For as long as the moment lasts, that hallowed, gracious time.

But no moment lasts forever, and it is not for twelve months a year that the bird of dawning singeth all night long. Darkness inevitably returns with all its shadows and ambiguities. The story of the birth of Jesus has been subjected to the most critical scrutiny by believers and unbelievers alike, and nowhere have the Nativity passages of Luke and Matthew been more rigorously and objectively analyzed than within the purview of biblical scholarship, where no fact or claim has been allowed to go unchallenged. The when, where, how of the Nativity have been for generations and continue to be the subject of endless conjecture.

Even the date of his birth is uncertain because Matthew and Luke do not agree with each other. Neither of them can be reconciled with the traditional view that he was born during the first year of the Christian era as it has come to be reckoned. Luke says he was born in the year when Cyrenius, the Roman governor of Syria, took a census of Palestine, whereas Matthew says it was during the reign of Herod the Great. The difficulty is that Cyrenius's census is known to have been taken in AD 6 and Herod died in 4 BC. Thus Jesus was born either six years later than has been generally supposed or at least four years earlier. And the place of his birth is equally debatable. Bethlehem is the town traditionally named King David's town, but that may have come about simply in order to bring history into line with the Old Testament prophecy that Bethlehem was where the Messiah as the Son of David was destined to come from. There are good reasons for believing that he may actually have been born in Nazareth.

And finally, the how of his birth, all the poetry that has grown up around it—the wise men and the star, the shepherds keeping watch over their flocks by night, and the hymn the angels sang. If someone had been there with a camera, would he have recorded any of it, or was the birth of Jesus no more if no less wonderful than any other birth? Whatever the answer, it can be based only on faith. There is no other way. The kind of objective truth a camera could have recorded is buried beneath the weight of two thousand years.

But there is of course another kind of truth. Whether he was born in 4 BC or AD 6, in Bethlehem or Nazareth, whether there were multitudes of the heavenly host to hymn the glory of it or just Mary and her husband—when the child was born the whole course of human history was changed. That is a truth as unassailable as any truth. Art, music, literature, Western culture itself with all its institutions and Western man's whole understanding of himself and his world—it is impossible to conceive how differently things would have turned out if that birth had not happened whenever, wherever, however it did. And there is a truth beyond that: For millions of people who have lived since, the birth of Jesus made possible not just a new way of understanding life but a new way of living it.

For better or worse, it is a truth that, for twenty centuries, there have been untold numbers of men and women who, in untold numbers of ways, have been so grasped by the child who was born, so caught up in the message he taught and the life he lived, that they have found themselves profoundly changed by their relationship with him. And they have gone on proclaiming, as the writers of the Gospels proclaimed before them, that through the birth of Jesus a life-giving power was released into the world which to their minds could have been no less than the power of God himself. This is the central truth that Matthew and Luke are trying to convey in their accounts of the Nativity. And it was a truth which no language or legend seemed too extravagant to convey. What the birth meant—meant to them, to the world—was the truth that mattered to them most and, when all is said and done . . . perhaps the only truth that matters to anyone.

17

Matthew and Luke's Gospels come ultimately from the same place that prayers do, from that dimension of the self where out of their own richest silence they sought to commune with Silence itself, to make themselves heard by it and to hear. "Faith is," said the author of the Epistle to the Hebrews, ". . . the conviction of things not seen," and their art is their prayer to be able to see and make seen.

When it comes to the birth of a child, we are all of us romantics. A new life, a new hope, innocence coming into an old and weary world—if there is beauty anywhere, surely it is here. And yet heaven knows when it comes to depicting other events in the life of Jesus, especially the events centered around his passion and death, again there is beauty, but other things too. Pain and contradiction, bitterness and despair. The body on the cross is a symbol of hope and innocence no less than the babe in the manger. Down through the centuries painters have not shrunk back from the fact that real blood ran down from the thorny crown, that the flesh was lacerated by scourging, the mouth open to the cry of dereliction—"My God, my God, why hast thou forsaken me?"—the face of the mother disfigured by grief as she held the corpse of her child on her knees. There is beauty too, the beauty of peace in the midst of agony, and of victory in the ashes of defeat. It is a beauty deep in shadow. But when it comes to the Nativity, there is no shadow. There is no attempt to represent the throes of Mary's labor or the bloody and howling entrance of the child into the winter world. In one form or another, the manger always appears as a place of beauty and holiness and never as a cold and cheerless symbol of the world's indifference. "Silent, night, holy night, all is calm, all is bright." Down through the ages there have been countless variations on this theme, but the theme is always the same. Not a hair of Mary's head is out of place. The baby has been washed and dried, the stable swept.

But if there is the beauty of what is majestic and powerful, there is the beauty also of what is humble and powerless. Like any child, Jesus as a child has one power only and that is the power to love and be loved which is of all powers the most powerful because it alone can conquer the human heart; at the same time it is of all powers the most powerless, because it can do nothing except by consent. It is of the very essence of love to leave us free to respond or not to respond because the moment it attempts to force our hand, it is no longer love but coercion, and what it elicits from us is no longer love but obedience. The greatest single argument against the existence of God is the presence of evil in the world, and to the degree that the Christian faith attempts to answer it, its answer is all tied up in this. The argument is simply stated: If there is a God who is both good and all powerful, why do terrible things happen in the world? Why does God allow us to murder and wage wars? Why does he allow us to remain indifferent to each other's needs so that the poor go uncared for and children starve and in a sense all of us go hungry if only for the peace and understanding that the world cannot give? If there is a God, why did he not with his great goodness make things right in the first place, or why does he not with his great power intervene in the affairs of the world to make things right at least in the second place, now? What Christianity in effect seems to say is that God could presumably do these things—could have turned us out perfectly as an inventor turns out a perfect invention or could step in when we get out of line and move us around like pawns on a chessboard. But as Christianity understands it, God does not want us related to him as an invention to an inventor or pawns to a cosmic kibitzer. He wants us related to him as children are related to their father. He wants us in other words to love him, and if our love is to be spontaneous and real, we must be free also not to love him with all its grim consequences of human suffering. Evil exists in the world not because God is indifferent or powerless or absent but because man is free, and free he must be if he is to love freely, free he must be if he is to be human.

Like any baby, Jesus as a baby does not judge or exhort or puzzle the world with his teaching. He makes no demands, threatens no punishment, offers no rewards. The world is free to take him or leave him. He does not rule the world from his mother's lap but, like any child, is himself at the mercy of the world.

In trying to say too much, piety always runs the risk of saying too little or saying it wrong, and the great pitfall of Christian art, especially when it tries to portray the birth of Christ, is sentimentalism. The stable becomes a painted backdrop, the floor a carpeted stage, the manger a prop lined with artificial straw. Neither the holiness nor the humanness of the moment is rendered so much as the schmaltz, and the Incarnation becomes merely a Christmas card with all the scandal taken out of it instead of what St. Paul called "a stumbling block to Jews and folly to Gentiles," instead of the proclamation that the Creator of the ends of the earth came among us in diapers.

Silent night, holy night. All is calm, all is bright. It is the calm before the storm, but it is no less calm for that, no less beautiful. The time will come soon enough to sorrow with him as the Man of Sorrows, but in the meanwhile it is enough that we rejoice in him as the Princeling of Peace. As long as he stays the babe in the manger, he asks us nothing harder than to love him and accept his love, and the temptation is thus to keep him a babe forever, for our sakes and for his sake too. Hence, perhaps, the inevitable stillness of Nativity paintings. Nothing moves. The very air is gold and unstirring, the angels caught like birds in a net. Time itself seems to have stopped, and the whole creation holds its breath as if for fear that otherwise time will start again and with it the long journey the child must take through time into darkness, and the faithful with him. As long as he is young, he seems to stand still, beyond the reach of time and its lengthening shadows.

For instance, when an angel appeared to Joseph in a dream and warned him of the wrath of Herod, Joseph took his wife and child to Egypt, but it is no furtive flight of refugees, no grim escape from the tyrant's sword. Mary and Jesus ride a donkey, and Joseph walks beside them. Mary wears her good clothes although in most versions she seems to have left her halo behind. Maybe it was an attempt to remain incognito or was just her hurry to leave. Joseph is walking with a staff because he is not getting any younger, and the baby is bundled up against the fresh air. It is a family holiday, a trip to the country, and if there is trouble ahead, it is a long way ahead. The sky is blue, and the baby has fallen asleep.

The same note is struck in the legendary story of Saint Christopher. Saint Christopher is carrying the child across a raging stream, and the deeper in he wades, the heavier the child becomes until finally he cries out, "Had I borne the whole world on my shoulders, the burden had not been heavier!" to which the child replies, "Christopher, thou hast not only borne all the world upon thee, but thou hast borne him that created the world and must bear the heaviness of its sin upon his shoulders." It is a dark word the child speaks and a dark journey he is embarked upon, but as with the flight into Egypt, the child is untouched by the darkness of it because again time has stopped, and the child we see is a child who for the moment is beyond the power of time to hurt. He rides the old saint's back like a child on a pony. He raises his hand to bless a world whose fateful heaviness he has yet to feel.

When he was twelve, Luke says, Mary and Joseph took him to Jerusalem for the Passover, and somewhere in the confusion they lost him. When they finally found him three days later, he was in the temple deep in debate with the venerable teachers of the Law. These were the very men who were to become his archenemies in days to come—the pillars of orthodoxy who were to see him as a threat to everything they held most sacred—but at this point they were all admiration, "amazed at his understanding and his answers." It is a very Jewish story—our son the theologian, the parents' discreet but fathomless pride in the accomplishments of their first-born. You can see it in Mary's face, in the way Joseph scratches his head in wonderment, in the rapt attention of the elders themselves, one of whom is checking out the boy's answers in a copy of the Torah. "[W]ist ye not that I must be about my Father's business?" (KJV) he asks, and he does not have a doubt in the world who that Father is. He will return to Jerusalem another day.

Whatever moments are to come, this moment is forever. Nothing that will come to be can make this moment otherwise.

Everything that ever happens in a life goes on being a part of that life, not just the thing that happens last. The man on the cross is also the babe in the manger, the child on his journeys, the boy in the temple. No man is such a prisoner of chronology but that his past and his future too are not a living part of his present, accessible to him in his dreams if nowhere else and accessible to us in our dreams about him. "Before Abraham was, I am," Jesus said. Before my time on earth ran out, I am on earth and this time is my time. Before darkness covered the whole land and the veil of the temple was rent, all is calm, all is bright. Before I was a man, I am a child, a God.

Not first the birth, and then the life, and then the death, but all three of them together, all three of them always impinging upon us at once. Let the last word about the child be a child's word. He has all of his life ahead of him and behind him too. If eternity is not endless time but the essence of all times combined, past, present and future, then it is in eternity that he stands, like the bird of dawning that singeth all night long.

3

MINISTRY

Glory to the newborn king

J esus, when he began his ministry, was about thirty years of age, Luke says. He is no longer the kingly child enthroned high above the world's power to do him harm and beyond the touch of time. The angels who attended his birth have vanished, and the magi have long since left their gifts at his feet and gone home. The star of Bethlehem has faded from view in the light of the hot, Near-Eastern sun. If the shepherds who kept watch over their flocks by night were once convinced that he was the Long-Expected One, the One by whom heaven and earth are named, they give no signs of remembering. The child has become a man, and, like all men, is caught up in time, in change and mortality. To understand him, we must understand the time he moved in and that moved in him. The difficulty is that this is just what we cannot do very satisfactorily.

Facts and figures abound, but what it was like to be a product of that distant time, to think as people thought then, to believe as they believed, to know no more and no less than they knew, is beyond our power because just as they were captives of their time, so we are captives of ours.

Palestine was a province of the Roman Empire, which allowed the Jews a measure of self-rule but maintained a strong military presence and kept them under close supervision. The Jews were divided into various sects. There were the Zealots, the fire-breathing nationalists who looked for the expulsion of Rome and the restoration of Jewish independence. There were semi-monastic sects like the Essenes who retreated to the wilderness around the Dead Sea in an effort to turn the clock back to the time of Israel's purity when life was comparatively simple and uncomplicated. There were the Pharisees who sought to reinterpret the ancient Law of Moses to meet the exigencies of a situation that had changed profoundly since Moses' day, and the Scribes, the scholars who worked out these reinterpretations which were eventually to become as binding as the Law. There were the ultra-conservative Sadducees who tended to shut their eyes to change in general and refused to reinterpret anything. What was good enough for Moses was good enough for them, and whereas the Pharisees believed in the resurrection of the dead, the Sadducees rejected it because it was not to be found in Scripture. There were the *Am-Hares*, or People of the Land, the unlettered commonality who did not so much hold views as they were simply swayed by them—sometimes one, sometimes another—and whose main business was just to survive as best they could the continual onslaughts of poverty and disease.

In all of these groups hope ran high that God would send a Messiah to redeem his chosen people, Israel, but this hope took many different forms, themselves indistinct and overlapping. Some dreamed that the Messiah would come as a warrior like King David to throw off the foreign rule. Others thought of him as a great priest like Melchizedek or a great prophet like Elijah. Somehow Jesus was a part of all this and all this a part of him, but no one can say just how or to what effect.

The writers of the Gospels make no attempt to show how he fitted into the religio-political complexities of first-century Israel but only how he fitted into the hearts of those who believed in him. They make no attempt either to depict his personality, to suggest the way he walked, talked, the kind of things that made him laugh, his attitude toward his friends, his family. There are only hints of these matters, to be read differently by each who reads them.

There seems to be a kind of sad humor about some of his parables—the man who tries to sleep through his friend's importunate midnight knocking; the rich man trying to squeeze into paradise like a camel through a needle's eye—and one can imagine him smiling as he told them, but maybe the smile is only our own. What seems to have made him angriest was hypocrisy and irrelevance, and thus it is the Pharisees who come in for his strongest attacks, the good people who should have known better. "You brood of vipers," he called them. "How can you speak good when you are evil?" When news was brought him that his friend Lazarus was dead, we are told that he wept, and at Gethsemane on the night of his arrest, the prospect of his own death shook him as it would shake any man. He sweated blood, the Gospel of Luke tells us, and prayed God to take the bitter cup from him if it was his will.

But there seem to have been happy moments too though the Gospels do not make much of them—the wedding at Cana where he saved the day by turning water into wine, the time he was out with the disciples on the Sea of Galilee and was lulled asleep by the rocking of the boat. Unlike John the Baptist, he was no grim ascetic but was accused of being a glutton and a drunk; and when the disciples of John asked him why he and his disciples did not fast, his answer was, "Can the wedding guests mourn as long as the bridegroom is with them?"

The author of the Epistle to the Hebrews describes him as "one who in every respect has been tempted as we are, yet without sinning": tempted to be a demagogue, a spellbinder, a mere humanitarian, we are told in the account of his encounter in the wilderness with Satan, who offered him all the kingdoms of the earth if he would only settle for them and no more; tempted to escape martyrdom as Peter urged him to, saying, "God forbid, Lord! This shall never happen to you," to which Jesus replied,

"Get behind me, Satan! You are a hindrance to me"; tempted, ultimately, to doubt the very faithfulness of God as he howls out his *Eloi, Eloi* from the cross.

And yet without sinning, Hebrews says. However great the temptation to abandon once and for all both his fellow humans and his God—who together he had good reason to believe had abandoned him—he never ceased to reach out to them in love, forgiving finally his own executioners. He addressed his cry of dereliction to a God who, in spite of everything, he believed to the end was near enough, and counted him dear enough, to hear it. The paradoxical assertion that Jesus was both fully man and in some way also fully God seems to many the unnecessary and obfuscating doctrine of later theologians, but the truth of the matter is that like all doctrines it was an experience first, in this case the experience of the simple folk who had actually known him. Having talked with him and eaten with him, having seen him angry, sad, merry, tired, and finally dead, they had no choice but to say that he was human even as they themselves were humans. But having found in him an undying power to heal and transform their lives, they had no choice but to say that he was God too if only because there was no other way of saying it.

If the doctrine of the divinity of Christ is paradoxical, it is only because the experience was paradoxical first. Much as we may wish it otherwise, reality seldom comes to us simple, logical, all of a piece. Humans are animal, we must say if we are honest, but they are also more than animal. In honesty we must say that too. If we are determined to speak the plain sense of our experience, we must be willing to risk the charge of speaking what often sounds like nonsense.

What we see of this extraordinary man we see only dimly and at the remove of centuries from a time we can never fully understand. Yet to read the New Testament with not just our eyes but our hearts and imagination open as well, is to catch a glimpse of a figure who from time to time we believe we are finally able to identify whether as Gentle Jesus Meek and Mild or Christ the Tiger, the teacher, the revolutionary, the merchant of dreams.

But even when we think we have come close to seeing him for who he truly was—the figure he cut, the face he wore—we must acknowledge always that what we have seen does not at most include who he was behind that face, the mystery of his inner life, of how he thought of himself and how he would have thought of us.

Did he think of himself as the Messiah, for instance? Some have argued that he did not, pointing to, among other things, what is often his curious ambivalence when the question is put to him directly. "Are you the one who is to come, or shall we look for another?" the disciples of John the Baptist ask him, to which his answer is, "Go and tell John what you hear and see," and when Caiaphas says, "Tell us if you are the Christ, the Son of God," his reply, according to Matthew, is the equally cryptic "You have said so."

On the other hand, it is possible that he was reluctant to accept the title simply because it was charged with chauvinistic associations from which he wished to disassociate himself. Mark, in any event, has Jesus answer Pilate's question with an unequivocal, "I am," and it is hard to see why they would have crucified him as a self-proclaimed Messiah with "Jesus of Nazareth, King of the Jews" nailed up over his head in three languages unless he had indeed proclaimed it. And it is hard to believe that his followers would have gone on proclaiming it about him unless they had heard it in some sense from his own lips. But even if that is true, it still leaves the question, in what sense? If he thought of himself as the Messiah, what kind of Messiah did he have in mind?

One thing at least seems clear. His role as he understood it was not to lead the people in glory but to suffer for them in love. "The Son of man came not to be served but to serve," he said, "and to give his life as a ransom for many." Again and again he strikes this note. The road that God has set before him is a road that involves great suffering, and suffering is to be the lot as well of all who choose to follow him on it. He makes no bones about this. "If any man would come after me, let him deny himself and take up his cross and follow me," he tells his disciples. And when a woman asks him to assure her sons places of prominence in heaven, he turns to them and asks, "Are you able to drink the cup that I am to drink?" If the guilty are to be saved, it is only by the suffering for them of the innocent, of the Messiah himself as the innocent one who shoulders the burden of their guilt.

Somewhere in the background of this there seems to stand a shadowy figure out of the book of Isaiah known as the Suffering Servant who is described in one of a series of poems as "despised and rejected of men; a man of sorrows and acquainted with grief," as one who "was wounded for our transgressions, he was bruised for our iniquities" so that "with his stripes we are healed" (KJV). The Gospels contain a number of echoes from these ancient poems including the opening words of Mark and the words spoken at the time of Jesus' baptism. Jesus' own view of himself seems to have been unmistakably influenced by them as when, on his return to the synagogue at Nazareth, the passage he chooses to read is from them, "The Spirit of the Lord GOD is upon me, because the LORD has anointed me to bring good tidings to the poor; he has sent me to bind up the broken-hearted, to proclaim liberty to the captives and recovering of sight to the blind."

The poor, the brokenhearted, the disinherited, the riffraff—from the beginning of his ministry these were the ones that Jesus particularly addressed himself to rather than to the ones who would have given him a more powerful following. Nothing he ever said strikes deeper chords than "Come to me, all who labor and are heavy laden, and I will give you rest," not that in a sense all people are not one way or another laboring and heavy laden under the burden of their own lives but that it is the down-trodden, the outcasts, who understand it best and are most apt to prick up their ears at the sound of his words. The rich, the respectable, the resourceful are tempted always to believe that they have no burden they cannot manage well enough on their own. It was the riffraff he spoke to, the riffraff who became his followers, his disciples even—tax collectors, whores, hicks—and when the Pharisees took him to task for this, his answer was, "Those who are well have no need of a physician, but those who are sick," and then, "I came not to call the righteous, but sinners."

And call them to what? What was the thrust of the message he carried, this strange and elusive man whom we can never either really know or escape knowing? What was the gospel, God's spiel, good news he gave his life to proclaiming, not just to Jews because "many shall come from the east and the west," as he told the Roman centurion, "and shall sit down with Abraham, and Isaac, and Jacob, in the kingdom of heaven"? (KJV)

To everybody who would listen then, what was his holy pitch? Not like the prophets, who always produced their credentials by telling the story of how God called them to be prophets in the first place and who always covered themselves by prefacing their words with "thus saith the Lord"; and not like the rabbis, who cited scriptural chapter and verse for everything they said; but with an utter and unqualified conviction of his power to speak on his own authority of even the highest and holiest things, he proclaimed the Kingdom of God.

He said the Kingdom was coming, a new order of things in which God's will was to be done on earth as it was done in heaven so that at last people would love their neighbors as themselves and God as their father. He said it was coming soon and was indeed already partly present in his own healing work of proclaiming it. He said that there was nothing people could do either to hasten it or prevent it, but that they were to work for it, pray for it, and above all be ready to receive it when the time came.

In his own way, John the Baptist had proclaimed something like this before him, but whereas John had proclaimed it as a prophet of doom using images like a threshing floor and a fan, or an axe ready to strike, and telling people they had to repent or else, Jesus proclaimed it as God's good gift which would be given whether people repented or not and pictured the experience of entering it as an experience of joy like attending a great feast or stumbling on buried treasure or finding a pearl of great price. This was what made his Good News good and also what made it new, this message from the stars that it was not just to the righteous that the Kingdom would come but to any of us however sinful who would only open our hearts to receive it.

You did not have to make yourself righteous first in order to qualify for admission—in fact by their very effort to fulfill the letter of the Law, the Pharisees were continually missing its spirit—but if you would only accept the gift of God's love in humility and faith, God himself would make you loving, which was, Jesus said, the fulfillment of all the law and the prophets.

Thus it was not by being good that people were to be saved, because by themselves that was just what they could not be. And when the rich young ruler called Jesus "Good Teacher," Jesus himself bridled under the epithet saying, "Why do you call me good? No one is good but God alone." It was not by good works that people had to win their way into the Kingdom, but like the Prodigal Son all they had to do was set their faces for home and God would be there to welcome them with open arms before they even had a chance to ask forgiveness for all the years of their prodigality.

But if good works are not the cause of salvation, they are nonetheless the mark and effect of it. If the forgiven ones do not become forgiving, the loved ones loving, then they are only deceiving themselves. "You will know them by their fruits," Jesus says, and here Gentle Jesus Meek and Mild becomes Christ the Tiger, becomes both at once, this stern and loving man. "Every tree that does not bear good fruit is cut down and thrown into the fire," he says, and Paul is only echoing him when he writes to the Galatians, "[T]he fruit of the Spirit is love, joy, peace, patience, kindness, goodness, faithfulness, gentleness, self-control; against such there is no law."

This then is the gospel that Jesus seems both to have proclaimed with his lips and lived with his life, not just preaching to the dispossessed of his day from a high pulpit, but coming down and acting it out by giving himself to them body and soul as if he actually enjoyed it—horrifying all Jericho by spending the night there not with the local rabbi, say, or some prominent Pharisee but with Zaccheus of all people, the crooked tax collector. When Simon the Pharisee laid into him for letting a streetwalker dry his feet with her hair, Jesus said, "I tell you her sins, which are many, are forgiven, for she loved much." It is no wonder that from the very start of his ministry the forces of Jewish morality and of Roman law were both out to get him because to him the only morality that mattered was the one that sprang from the forgiven heart like fruit from the well-watered tree, and the only law he acknowledged as ultimate was the law of love.

A man who was of all men most human yet like no man seems to have seen himself as divine. A Man of Sorrows who at the end of his life said, "These things I have spoken to you, that my joy may be in you, and that your joy may be full." A man who ate and drank and wept with sinners but who lashed out against sin with a violence that can still make the blood run cold; who was tempted to fall but never fell; who went down in defeat only to rise up in victory—it is no wonder that we can never fully know him or be sure even of what little we think we do know, including the content of these pages. As Albert

Schweitzer wrote at the end of *The Quest of the Historical Jesus*, "He comes to us as One unknown, without a name, as of old, by the lakeside. He came to those men who knew Him not. He speaks to us the same word: 'Follow thou me!' and sets us to the tasks which He has us to fulfil for our time. He commands, and to those who obey Him, whether they be wise or simple, He will reveal Himself in the toils, the conflicts, the sufferings, which they shall pass through in His fellowship, and, as an ineffable mystery, they shall learn in their own experience Who He is."

Follow thou me. Follow him deep enough to catch at least a glimpse of that face that changed the face of all subsequent history. Follow him as far as the banks of the Jordan where John the Baptist sees him coming and says, "Behold, the Lamb of God, who takes away the sin of the world."

"I need to be baptized by you," John says, but Jesus answers, "Let it be so now; for thus it is fitting . . ."; and as he answers, his lips part in a smile of profound gaiety as though at the absurdity of the one who takes away the sin of the world receiving on his own head the baptism of repentance for the forgiveness of sins.

Or perhaps it is the smile of the Renaissance prince who receives at the hands of a vassal a gift which in his great wealth he does not need but which he more than pays for by the exquisite courtesy with which he is pleased to accept it. Thus it is fitting, he says. Or maybe it is the smile of a man who at the start of a journey which he knows will end in his death shows by his smiling how he knows too that the death he journeys to is as nothing compared with the life that will spring from it like wheat from a buried seed.

The Baptism in Jordan was the door through which Jesus passed into his ministry because it seems to have been at this moment that he first knew himself fully to be the Anointed One, which is what Messiah means in Hebrew, *Christos* in Greek.

Gathering his camel's hair garment at the knee to keep it from getting wet, John pours the water on his head from a chalice as the Holy Spirit descends upon Jesus like a dove, and a voice from heaven, echoing the first of the Suffering Servant poems, says, "Thou art my beloved son; with thee I am well pleased." Jesus seems to have broken with John at some later date, not baptizing his followers as John did, but from the earliest stages of the Christian movement, the sacrament was reinstituted as a symbol of dying to the old and rising to the new, thus becoming the door through which all believers must pass.

If in the scenes of his birth and childhood Jesus seems to be always standing still on the banks of time which never touches him, in these scenes of his ministry he is caught up in the relentless flow of it. If there are moments of repose now, they are moments salvaged in the midst of turbulent activity. One pictures him continually moving forward, continually speaking, as though he knows that there is no moment to lose.

He is passing along by the Sea of Galilee when he sees Andrew and Peter casting their nets into the water; and without preface or explanation he calls out to them on the run, "Follow me and I will make you become fishers of men," as they rise to their feet in their small green boat, and one of them reaches out to take his hand. Their faces are grave, the bodies of the disciples tense as they prepare to leap to the shore to follow him.

With the jerky haste of an old newsreel, Jesus flickers across the light-struck Galilean landscape. Parables and beatitudes fill the air about him like scratches on an old film—Blessed are the meek, the poor, the pure in heart—and people throng about him to be healed. A woman stretches out her hand to touch the hem of his garment as he goes hurrying by. At Cana he stops long enough to go to a wedding, and when his mother tells him the wine has given out, his answer is impatient and time-haunted. "My hour has not yet come," he says, but he takes time to do her bidding anyway and makes wine out of the six great jars of water.

In Samaria he stops at a well because he is tired and thirsty from his journeying. There is a woman drawing water. One imagines her with one knee raised to display a slender ankle. Jesus does not have to be clairvoyant to see her for what she is. She is transparent, but she does not seem to mind being seen through.

The two disciples who are lurking in the background are clearly dismayed by her unseemly behavior—one of them plucks at his beard and the other averts his frowning gaze—but Jesus wastes no time on moral exhortation. Since their paths may never cross again, he must speak to her of what matters most while he still has the chance. "Every one who drinks of this water will thirst again," he tells her, "but whoever drinks of the water that I shall give him will never thirst." Then his sense of the inexorable passage of time rises in him again, and, "The hour is coming," he says, "when neither on this mountain nor in Jerusalem will you worship the Father." Then, "But the hour is coming and now is when the true worshippers will worship the Father in spirit and truth." The hour is so nearly at hand that in a sense it is at hand already: the hour of the Kingdom's coming when this insouciant lady and everyone else must make their fateful decision for it or against it. Which way the lady herself finally decided, the Gospel of John never tells us, but the part of her conversation with Jesus that appears to have impressed her most was his strange ability to tell her about the five men she had married and the rather less formal relationship she had entered into with the one she was currently keeping house with. This is at least the burden of the report she carried back to the city when she left him. She had met this perfectly marvelous fortuneteller, she informed them, and then added almost as an afterthought that it was possible he might be the Messiah too. The chances seem to be that it is as a fortuneteller that he has interested her most, however, and that if she makes it to the Kingdom in the end, it will be less her own doing than the doing of the Holy One, who has a soft spot in his heart for ladies with slender ankles.

Again and again as their accounts of Jesus' ministry unfold, the Gospels convey in spite of themselves that it was something less than the brilliant success that the extraordinary circumstances of his birth seemed to foreshadow. He tells parables that are simplicity itself yet even the people closest to him often fail to understand them. He miraculously feeds a crowd of five thousand that comes to see him, but there is no record that he made a single convert. When he went back to Nazareth, his friends said, "He is beside himself," and there is reason to believe that his own mother and brothers were confused too.

On a number of occasions he chides the disciples for their lack of faith, those men who of all men had most reason to be faithful. When he pictured the end of the world and the coming of the Son of man in his glory and predicted that "this generation will not pass away till all these things take place," all you can say is that, as things turned out, he was wrong.

And finally there was Lazarus, the friend from Bethany whom he loved and whose sisters he loved. When word was brought to him that Lazarus was ill, he said, "This illness is not unto death," and when on the contrary it killed him, Jesus was still able to speak words which his followers to this day treasure as among the most precious he ever spoke: "I am the resurrection and the life; he who believes in me, though he die, yet shall he live, and whoever lives and believes in me shall never die." But when he went to Bethany and actually faced the sisters in their terrible grief, he could find for the moment no more such brave and hopeful words. "He was deeply moved in spirit," the evangelist writes, and then that shortest, bluntest verse in the entire New Testament: "Jesus wept."

If we could understand all that lay behind those tears, we would understand much about him, more maybe than it is well for us to understand; but to the degree that he was, whatever else, a human being like ourselves, we understand at least something. It was presumably the naked fact itself that staggered him there in Bethany—death not as a distant darkness that his great faith was light enough to see him through; death not as a universal condition; but death as *this* death and darkness which he saw written across the swollen faces of the two women who stood there before him. Whatever Jesus may at other moments have seen as rising bright as hope beyond it, at this particular moment death was a darkness he had no heart to see beyond. Maybe it was more than that. "Could not he who opened the eyes of the blind have kept this man from dying?" some of the bystanders muttered in his hearing. It is hard not to believe that in the abyss of his being, Jesus was asking himself the same dark question.

It is hard not to believe that it was for himself as well as Lazarus that he wept there. And that what he must have been tempted to see as the defeat and failure of everything that he had given his life to proclaim was, in some unspeakable measure, the failure and defeat even of his God. Even when he goes to the tomb and raises his old friend up, you feel that the death and the defeat of it are not entirely undone. Jesus stands with one arm raised crying, "Lazarus, come out!" but what has appeared in the doorway of the stone tomb is a shrouded ruin. It is not a living man who prepares to come out again into the unsparing light of day but a living corpse.

If death was to be truly defeated, it was only by dying himself that Jesus believed he could defeat it. If he was to reach the hearts of men, it was only by suffering his own heart to be broken on their behalf that he believed he could reach them. To heal the sick and restore sight to the blind; to preach good news to the poor and liberty to the captives; to wear himself out with his endless teaching and traveling the whole length and breadth of the land—it had not worked because it was not enough. There had to be more. "He set his face to go to Jerusalem," the Gospel says, and it was a journey from which he seems to have known that he would both never return and return always even unto the end of time and beyond.

4

LAST SUPPER

Gentle Jesus . . .
the merchant of dreams

For all of us there finally comes not just a last time but a whole calendar of last times—the last time we see our child, our friend. The last time we take a walk along the beach or see the rain fall. The last time we make love or write a letter, build a fire, hear our name spoken. It is part of the mercy of things that we rarely know when each last time comes, are never sure when we are saying good-bye for good. Even the old man dying in his bed believes that he will feel the touch of a human hand again before he's done or hear the drawing of the blind, smell breakfast, drift off one more time into an old man's dozing. For some it is given to know—the criminal watching the sun come up on the morning of his execution, the suicide writing his note—but even for them there must always be the wild hope that somehow a miracle will happen to save them.

But for Jesus because he believed he had to die in order to save the world, there could be no hope for anything from the world to save him from dying. God was the power that he believed filled and sustained him, but it was God who had made him powerless. The miracle was to be that there would be no miracle. When it came time for him to eat his last meal with his friends, he knew it was his last. He was to be spared nothing.

For all their tendency to propagandize and prettify, the Gospels, at the same time, disarm us again and again with their helpless honesty. If there are certain events that they cannot tell without improving on them a little with each retelling—the birth, for instance—there are others that almost in spite of themselves they seem unable to tell except in the curt monosyllables of fact. There are the various blunderings of the disciples, for instance, or the crucifixion where even John resists the temptation to put a long farewell into the mouth of the crucified one; or the resurrection which takes place in confusion and half-light when everybody who should have been there is off somewhere else. And the same thing holds true in their account of this final meal that he lived to eat with his friends.

It would have been only human to picture it as an unusually successful affair with the disciples rising to the occasion as never before and Jesus presiding as the perfect host, serene and radiant and at peace to the last. But that is not the way the Gospels present it at all.

True to form, the disciples start bickering about which of them is to be regarded as the greatest. In that very room where they had every reason to know that something fateful and tragic was about to happen to the leader they swore they loved, it is their own fate they are worried about as they set about jockeying for position. "[L]et the greatest among you become as the youngest, and the leader as one who serves," Jesus says, and you can hear the weariness in his voice as he says it, wondering if it can be possible after all he has tried to show them both with his words and with his life that they have still missed the whole point of everything.

Peter is the one of them who shows some signs of understanding when he protests, "Lord, I am ready to go with you to prison and to death," but not even in him does Jesus see grounds for much hope. "Peter, the cock will not crow this day, until you three times deny that you know me," he tells him, and you can hear the silence that settles over the table like a mist. Not only will Peter deny him, Jesus says, but one of them sitting there is going to betray him, and no sooner are the words out of his mouth than their recriminations begin. As a moment before, when they wanted to know which of them was to be the hero of the piece, now they want to know which will be the villain. Nothing is more important to them than that the score be kept. It is to the disciple sitting nearest him, the disciple whom we are told he especially loved, that Jesus identifies the one he means. "It is he to whom I shall give this morsel when I have dipped it," he whispers, and the one who takes it from his hands and slips out into the night is Judas, the son of Simon Iscariot.

Jesus knows that it is their last supper together and he makes no secret of it. "This is my body," he says, picking up the bread. He breaks it in two and gives it away to them—"take . . . eat. . . ." And then the wine. "This is my blood which is poured out," he tells them. "Drink of it all of you," and while the stain of it is still dark on their lips, he says, "I shall not drink again of this fruit of the vine until that day when I drink it new with you in my Father's kingdom."

It is the great Messianic Feast to take place beyond time that he is speaking of, but he must have had a hard time believing in it there in that stuffy room full of frightened Jews.

When he first sent them out as disciples, he reminds them, he told them to take no purse or bag or sandals, nothing to arm themselves with against the world, "but now let him who has a purse take it, and likewise a bag, and let him who has no sword sell his mantle and buy one." This side of paradise there is to be no paradise, and this side of the "peace of God, which passeth all understanding" there is to be no peace that they are likely to understand. They are going to have to fight fire with fire, he tells these feckless men, and if it is to be a fire that lights the way to truth, it will also kindle the blaze of their own cruel martyrdom. He promises them no less.

And then they sing a hymn, the Gospels say. Their mouths spit dry, not one of them with heart enough to carry a tune. Their voices thin and quavering as they try to keep their spirits up, they belt out some crazy, holy song and leave for the Mount of Olives where Jesus says, "You will all fall away."

Whatever else it was not, it was at least human, this final feast. One hardly knows whether to laugh or to weep. They were no better and no worse than they had always been, the twelve feasters. They were themselves to the end. And if there is a kind of black comedy about them, the way the Gospels paint the scene, there is a kind of battered courage about them too. Even though they knew what was coming, knew even what their own unedifying part in it was to be, they stuck to their guns, all but one of them. And in the long run, if not the short, they stuck to Jesus too. God makes his saints out of fools and sinners because there is nothing much else to make them out of. God makes his Messiah out of a fierce and fiercely gentle man who spills himself out, his very flesh and blood, as though it is only a loaf of bread and a cup of sweet red wine that he is spilling.

Jesus sits at a table. He is surrounded by his twelve friends. In our mind's eye we can see them caught unawares with their hands frozen in the middle of gestures, their faces unguarded and lost between expressions. One of them stares up at the ceiling with a look of tipsy bravado, and another shakes his fist at a friend across from him who seems to have his mind elsewhere, as to a degree all of them do. Hardly a one of them is paying any attention to Jesus. Their eyes are open, but there is something oddly sightless about them so that even the one or two who are looking at him do not seem to see him. The beloved disciple has fallen asleep with his chin resting on the table. Jesus has his right hand resting lightly on the man's forehead.

The dark shadow of Jesus' lips suggests the shadow of a smile or maybe he is starting to say something. He is about to say, "This is my blood." Perhaps he is also holding a bit of bread and is about to identify Judas by handing it to him. It is possible that Judas may be the one looking up at the ceiling and only pretending to be tipsy and brave as maybe the beloved disciple is only pretending to be asleep. In any case, it is Jesus who dominates the scene.

But Jesus is more fully present at that table than any of the rest of them. The disciples all have the air of men lost in their own thoughts, but Jesus belongs totally to this time, this place. His gaze begins to move slowly from face to face around the table—those great heavy-lidded eyes that have seen everything, the bearded mouth, the porous stone cheeks with pools of darkness in them. You can see in his face both how it was that these men had had no choice but to follow when he first called them to him and how it is that they cannot bring themselves to look directly at him now. There is a dreamlike quality about the scene: a dream that hangs heavy in the memory long after waking, that cries out to be understood and at the same time is unyielding and impenetrable.

The Last Supper can be seen as madness and hallucination. Jesus is a madman. He sits cringing at a small table covered with a white cloth. With one hand he is clutching a loaf of bread to him as though his life depends on it, as though there is nothing anywhere in the known universe that does not depend on it.

Jesus can be seen as paranoid. He believes he is God and that the world is out to get him. Centuries may pass before it is possible to assess the full extent of the disaster. If Jesus was not the Messiah, then he was a lunatic who thought he was. It is difficult to see how there can be any middle ground.

In his own way, Paul would have perhaps understood either view, Paul as the only one who ever dared speak of the foolishness of God, of the crucifixion itself as folly, of the folly of his own preaching. If the world is sane, then Jesus is mad as a hatter and the Last Supper is the Mad Tea Party. The world says, Mind your own business, and Jesus says, There is no such thing as your own business. The world says, Follow the wisest course and be a success, and Jesus says, Follow me and be crucified. The world says, Drive carefully—the life you save may be your own—and Jesus says, Whoever would save his life will lose it, and whoever loses his life for my sake will find it. The world says, Law and order, and Jesus says, Love. The world says, *get* and Jesus says, *give*. In terms of the world's sanity, Jesus is crazy as a coot, and anybody who thinks he can follow him without being a little crazy too is laboring less under a cross than under a delusion.

"We are fools for Christ's sake," Paul says, faith says—the faith that ultimately the foolishness of God is wiser than the wisdom of men, the lunacy of Jesus saner than the grim sanity of the world. Through the eyes of faith too, the Last Supper, though on one level a tragic farewell and failure—farce even— is also, at its deepest level, the foreshadowing of great hope and the bodying forth of deep mystery. Frail, fallible, foolish as he knows the disciples to be, Jesus feeds them with himself. The bread is his flesh, the wine his blood, and they are all of them including Judas to eat and drink him down. They are to take his life into themselves and come alive with it, to be his hands and feet in a world where he no longer has hands and feet, to feed his lambs. "Do this in remembrance of me," Paul quotes him as saying. In eating the bread and drinking the wine, they are to remember him, Jesus tells them, and to remember him not merely in the sense of letting their minds drift back to him in the dim past but in the sense of recalling him to the immediate present. They are to remember him the way when we remember people we love who have died, our hearts kindle to the living reality of their presence.

In its fullest sense, remembering is far more than a long backward glance, and in its fullest sense the symbol of bread and wine is far more than symbol.

It is part of the mystery of any symbol always to contain something of the power of the thing symbolized just as it is more than a mere piece of painted cloth that makes your pulse quicken when you come upon your country's flag in a foreign land. When in remembrance of Jesus, the disciples ate the bread and drank the wine, it was more than mere bread and wine they were consuming, and for all the tragic and ludicrous battles Christians have fought with each other for centuries over what actually takes place at the Mass, the Eucharist, Communion, or whatever they call it, they would all seem to agree that something extraordinary takes place. Even if the priest is a fraud, the bread a tasteless wafer, the wine not wine at all but temperance grape juice, the one who comes to this outlandish meal in faith may find there something to feed his deepest hunger, a new life to bring him alive.

Or of course he may find nothing. Unlike magic whereby if you say "abracadabra" right the spell will always work, religion does not make anything always work; and faith cannot be sure of things happening the way it wants because it is God who makes things happen the way God wants. Faith can only wait in hope and trust. Sometimes God makes himself known by his presence, sometimes by his absence, and for both faith and unfaith the absence of God is dark and menacing.

"What you are going to do," Jesus says to Judas, "do quickly."

What Judas is going to do, he does in a garden, but though he goes about it as quickly as he can, there is a little time to wait before he gets there. It is night, and they are all tired. Jesus tells them, "My soul is very sorrowful, even to death," and then asks the disciples to stay and watch for him while he goes off to pray. One thinks of the stirring and noble way others have met their deaths—the equanimity of Socrates as he raised the hemlock to his lips, the exaltation of Joan at the stake. Jesus is like neither. Maybe it is because it is to the ones who are most fully alive that death comes most unbearably. His prayer is, "Abba; Father, all things are possible to thee; remove this cup from me; yet not what I will, but what thou wilt"—this tormented muddle of a prayer which Luke says made him sweat until it "became like great drops of blood falling down upon the ground." He went back to find some solace in the company of his friends then but found them all asleep when he got there. "The spirit indeed is willing, but the flesh is weak," he said, and you feel that it was to himself he was saying it as well as to them.

From the expression on their faces, you can tell that they are having good dreams. You can imagine Jesus hesitating a moment before he waked them. You can imagine the temple guards chinking across the grass in their armor and one of the disciples cutting off the ear of the high priest's slave with his sword. Matthew has Jesus chide the disciple for his brashness, and Luke, going one step further, has him touch the ear and heal it, but Mark, writing earliest, gives no indication that Jesus had time even to notice.

All three of them, however, agree about Judas. It was Judas who led the authorities to the garden a little way east of Jerusalem, and it was Judas who signaled to them which of the men standing there in the dark was Jesus. The way he signaled, of course, was by going up to him and kissing him, and when Dante came to write his *Inferno*, it was because of this kiss that he placed Judas in the nethermost circle of hell, his torment being to spend eternity in the icy Lake of Cocytus while Satan, winged like a bat, gnaws at his frozen flesh.

Judas seems frozen at least in time as he leans forward with one hand on Jesus' chest, their beards just touching. There is something tentative in the way he goes about it as if for a moment he is not sure that he has found the right man or that, having found him, he can remember what his kiss is supposed to signal. We cannot see his face very well, just a part of his profile—the lines on his forehead and the corner of one eye, the curve of his cheek. It is easier to condemn a man to the nethermost circle of hell when you cannot see such things too clearly.

Jesus' eyes are closed, and he seems to be unsteady on his feet, leaning a little backward and clutching onto his robe. He could be Dostoevsky's Father Zossima, who said, "Fathers and teachers, I ponder, 'What is hell?' I maintain that hell is the suffering of being unable to love." He has his left hand raised in benediction.

The soldiers are there with their swords and lanterns. The high priest's slave is whimpering over his wounded ear. There can be no doubt in Jesus' mind what the kiss of Judas means, but it is Judas that he is blessing, and Judas that he is prepared to go out and die for now. Judas is only the first in a procession of betrayers two thousand years long. If Jesus were to exclude him from his love and forgiveness, to one degree or another he would have to exclude us all.

Maybe this is all in the mind of Jesus as he stands with his eyes closed, or possibly there is nothing in his mind at all. As he feels his friend's lips graze his cheek for an instant, maybe he feels nothing else. It is another of his last times. On this last evening of his life he has eaten his last meal, and this is the last time that he will ever feel the touch of another human being except in torment. It is not the Lamb of God and his butcher who meet here, but two old friends embracing in a garden knowing that they will never see one another again.

5

CRUCIFIXION

This is my body . . .
This is my blood.

By the late Middle Ages Christian piety had evolved a detailed tradition about what happened to Jesus on his way from the trial before Pilate, the Roman procurator, to the site of his execution and finally his grave. The Stations of the Cross as they have come to be known represent the various incidents along that somber route: Jesus sentenced to death, receiving his cross, stumbling three times under the weight of it and then a passerby compelled to shoulder it the rest of the way for him; Jesus meeting his mother, meeting a woman named Veronica, who wiped his face with her veil which ever afterward bore the bloody imprint of his face upon it; Jesus saying to the women of Jerusalem, "Do not weep for me, but weep for yourselves and your children"; Jesus stripped of his garments, nailed to the cross, dying, laid in his tomb.

There are fourteen stations all told, and they are sometimes found carved or painted around the walls of churches so that especially during Lent and Holy Week the devout can move from one to another in meditation and prayer. Some of the incidents are entirely legendary—the meetings with Veronica and Mary, for instance—and some are to be found in the New Testament although by and large there are few such details about the road to Golgotha there. But there is of course nothing that occurred during those last few hours of Jesus' life, and nothing that the mind of faith can imagine having occurred, that has not been the subject of endless conjecture and innumerable works of art.

Before sending him off to his crucifixion, Pilate had Jesus scourged. It was a not uncommon practice at the time, especially in the case of criminals who were not Roman citizens. The Greek word found in the Gospels for scourge suggests that what was used may have been the *flagra*, which were iron chains ending in little metal balls or cords knotted over small bones at the ends, or it may have been a knot made of leather thongs, the *horrible flagellum* that Horace refers to in his *Satires*. In either case it was not unusual for the criminal to die under this preliminary punishment, thus being spared the greater one to follow. Jesus was not so fortunate and paintings show his naked flesh lacerated with the crimson drops of his blood falling from brow to groin like a mantilla.

The sentence passed, the scourging done, Jesus is given the cross to carry on his own shoulders to the hill of his execution like Hitler's Jews being forced to dig their own common grave before the bullets mowed them down at the lip of it. This "station" has been caught in silk on an embroidered English chasuble, the sleeveless vestment worn by a priest at the celebration of the Mass. Jesus is bent nearly double under the weight, and his eyes are glazed and staring like the eyes of a man set to a test of strength that he knows he will fail. The great load rests mainly on his shoulders, and his right arm is draped limply over the vertical shaft. One soldier seems to be trying to help him to his feet from behind while two others have their arms raised to bludgeon him forward. A fourth holds a trumpet to his silken lips, and all about them the air is stitched with gold as the procession starts to mount the Via Dolorosa of a fifteenth-century priest's finery.

Weakened almost beyond endurance by the ordeal of the scourge, Jesus is unable to carry his burden very far, and they seize one Simon of Cyrene.

Cyrene was a town on the northern coast of Africa opposite Crete, and some have held that Simon was black. Convinced that Jesus was a purely spiritual being whose human body was only an illusion, and horrified by the claim that he had actually suffered material pain at Calvary, the second-century Gnostics held that as soon as Simon shouldered the cross, Jesus magically transformed the man into his own likeness so that it was Simon

71

who was crucified when the time came while Jesus stood on the sidelines mocking the executioners. We are Gnostics ourselves when in excessive veneration of the godness of Jesus we shy away from his humanness, from the fact that like the rest of us he did not just have a body but was a body, a body that he might never have been able to drag another step farther if Simon of Cyrene had not been strong-armed into shouldering the cross for him.

You see something of the same gnostic tendency at work in the ghostly imprint of Jesus' face on Veronica's veil. The lips parted in a sigh of exhaustion and grief but the features classically handsome and unmarred. It looks like a tragic mask which the great actor wore while the play called for it, but underneath which he remained serene and untouched. It is not hard to sympathize with the Gnostics in their heresy. There is something in all of us that wants God, if we have one, to be beyond the reach of suffering. If God is to save us, he must himself stand safely on the bank lest he be caught up and swept away with the rest of us.

Christian orthodoxy, on the other hand, remembers again the Suffering Servant of Isaiah whom Jesus himself remembered and whose face is described as "marred beyond human semblance." For Jesus, as the Suffering Servant, the Divine Actor was so caught up in his holy part that the two became inseparable, and the gnostic Christ who only masqueraded as a man of sorrows becomes the Jesus of the classic creeds who was as fully human as he was fully divine so that when Veronica wiped his bloody face with her veil, it was a real man's face that left its stamp upon it, and real blood that was shed.

An anonymous African craftsman captures the humanity in a carving of his head only a few inches high. It is crowned with thorns, a black Christ carved out of some dark wood that has been polished and mellowed to a soft sheen. You ache to run your fingers down the bridge of the nose and the great, full lips; to trace the cool plane of the cheeks where the swirl of the grain has become the track of dried tears, the scar running down into one eyebrow where the wood has cracked. There are no words for saying all that shines out of that face. Compassion, beauty, sorrow, majesty, love—they are so freighted with meaning that they finally flounder. What the carving wordlessly tells us is simply all there is to tell about what it means to be black, what it means to be human, what it means to be God.

Finally the crucifixion itself. It was a Roman punishment, not a Jewish one, and whatever the connivance of the Jews may have been, it was the Romans who sentenced him to it and carried it out. It was a punishment for slaves and considered an outrage if inflicted on a Roman citizen. Usually the cross was not very high and constructed in the shape of a T. The condemned man was hoisted onto it, with his hands nailed or tied to the crossbar and his feet to the upright. Since the weight would have quickly torn through the hands, the body was supported by a peg between the thighs or possibly some kind of support beneath the feet. Death was usually a long time coming. Cramps started in the muscles of the forearms and then spread into the whole upper body, the abdomen, the legs. With this enormous burden on the heart, the pulse was inevitably slowed and the blood carried less and less oxygen to the lungs so that the victim slowly suffocated. Poisoned by waste matter that the heart was no longer strong enough to eliminate, the muscles were affected by spasms that caused excruciating pain. The ordeal often lasted as long as two or three days before the criminal finally ran out of strength and breath and died. Jesus was fortunate in surviving only a few hours.

"God so loved the world," John writes, "that he gave his only Son, that whoever believes in him should not perish but have eternal life." That is to say that God so loved the world that he gave his only Son even to this obscene horror; so loved the world that in some ultimately indescribable way and at some ultimately immeasurable cost he gave the world himself. Out of this terrible death, John says, came eternal life not just in the sense of resurrection to life after death but in the sense of life so precious even this side of death that to live it is to stand with one foot already in eternity. To participate in the sacrificial life and death of Jesus Christ is to live already in his kingdom. This is the essence of the Christian message, the heart of the Good News, and it is why the cross has become the chief Christian symbol. A cross of all things—a guillotine, a gallows— but the cross at the same time as the crossroads of eternity and time, as the place where such a mighty heart was broken that the healing power of God himself could flow through it into a sick and broken world.

It was for this reason that of all the possible words they could have used to describe the day of his death, the word they settled on was "good." Good Friday.

The man on the cross was a man of flesh, but he was also the WORD made flesh, as John writes it in the great prologue to his Gospel, the Word that "became flesh and dwelt among us, full of grace and truth." The Creator himself comes to dwell within his own creation, the Eternal within the temporal, the Invulnerable within the wound. It is as if Shakespeare could somehow have entered the world of *Hamlet*, say, the dramatist descending from the infinite dimensions of reality into the dimensionlessness of his own drama, becoming a character in his own plot although he well knows its tragic denouement and submitting himself to all its limitations so that he can burst them asunder when the time comes and lead a tremendous *exeunt* by which his whole *dramatis personae* will become true persons at last.

Something like this is what seems to be suggested by a curious modern sculpture which shows a wooden Jesus partially framed in a wooden rectangle. He has one arm stretched out horizontally through the frame into darkness, the hand pierced by a long vertical nail. This impaled, projecting hand is the outerness of it, the drama of it, and the pain. Within the frame is the innerness of it, the true heart of the dramatist which is both in the pain and beyond it. The face of Jesus is stern as death but alive and at peace. He is contemplating the palm of the other hand as though reading in it the play within the play, the destiny of destiny itself.

The outer pain, the inner peace—in depicting the crucifixion the artists tend always to emphasize one at the expense of the other. Only the greatest of them manage somehow to do justice to them both, like a twelfth-century crucifix where the cross has been lost, and all that remains is the body. With his arms winged out wide and his head bent, Jesus is dying but at the same time flying through the royal purple night. He looks Semitic with the shape of his nose, the cut of his beard, the way he has somehow shrugged off his cross. He is Abraham, Shylock, Dreyfus, the Baal Shem. He is a Jew here, all Jews.

"You shall be to me a kingdom of priests and a holy nation," God told Moses on Mount Sinai. "These are the words you shall speak to the children of Israel." Right from the beginning the trouble was that Israel had no taste for being a kingdom of priests but chose rather to be a nation like any other nation, a power among powers. Israel's whole tragic history can be read as an attempt to escape its holy calling and the terrible price exacted of it for doing so. Again and again it tried by playing international politics to make its weight felt in history only to be again and again decimated by history. The northern kingdom fell to Assyria in the eighth century BC, and in the sixth the Babylonians laid waste to Jerusalem in the south, burning Solomon's Temple and carrying the leaders off into captivity. For two hundred years afterwards the Persians held sway until in the fourth century Alexander the Great conquered Darius, and Israel became part of an empire, first under the Ptolomies, then under the Seleucids. After a brief period of independence, a civil war broke out between the two contending priest kings, and when one of them called on Rome to intervene in his behalf, Pompey marched into Jerusalem with the Roman eagles, captured the second temple, massacred some twelve thousand Jews, and made all Palestine a tributary of Rome.

Throughout all these centuries there were always the prophets thundering out at king and people to remember their ancient mission to be the kingdom of priests that God had called them to be, but each time the prophetic cry went largely unheeded, and each time Israel went down to another defeat with only a remnant of the pious left to be, as Isaiah put it, a green branch growing out of a hewn stump. Remnant led to remnant until finally, in terms of New Testament faith, the remnant became just Jesus and his twelve disciples. When the last of the disciples abandoned him, the remnant became just Jesus himself.

The kingdom of priests was reduced at last to this One, who was both priest and sacrifice, and so it is Israel itself that hangs there on the cross, the suffering one who was "bruised for our iniquities; upon him was the chastisement that made us whole."

Jesus is all Jews and in a sense also the only Jew as he hovers there in the purple sky. It is out of his passion that the Church will be born as the new Israel, a kingdom of priests at last. It is through his intercession that at the end of history the holy city, New Jerusalem, will come down out of heaven like a bride adorned for her husband.

Our age is full of people for whom the language of religious faith is a dead language and its symbols empty, for whom the figure of Jesus is vague and remote as a figure in a dream, powerless except for the power to stir the deepest intuitions and longings of the human heart—if ever there was a man worth dying with and dying for, this is he. If ever there should turn out unbelievably to be a God of love willing to search for men even in the depths of evil and pain, the face of Jesus is the face we would know him by.

Down through the ages the great Pietàs of Western art show the dead body of Jesus lying across the lap of his mother. The one who said that he was the light of the world has gone out like a match. The one who they said was the hope of the world is himself now hopeless.

There is reason to suspect that Mary never fully understood what her son was about and would have persuaded him to give it up if she could. Jesus never had much time for her, and when they came to him once to say that his mother was waiting outside, he told them that whoever did the will of his Father in heaven, that was his mother. Only on the cross did he seem to focus clearly on who she was and on the depths of her need. He told the disciple he loved most to look after her when he was gone and told her that from now on the disciple would be the son to her that he himself had had no time to be, what with a world to save, a death to die. He spoke to her more like her father than like her child, so that in losing him she lost a child and father both.

There is an ivory diptych that has the crucifixion on one panel and the entombment on the other, and the way the diptych is made, you can close it up like a book and fasten it with a clasp. One can imagine that at the end Mary was ready to close once and for all the book of her son's bewildering life and to let them roll up the great stone to seal it.

6

RESURRECTION

The cross as the crossroads
of eternity and time

On the day after Jesus died, Matthew says, "the chief priests and the Pharisees gathered before Pilate and said, 'Sir, we remember how that impostor said, while he was still alive, "After three days I will rise again." Therefore order the sepulcher to be made secure until the third day, lest his disciples go and steal him away, and tell the people, "He has risen from the dead," and the last fraud will be worse than the first.' Pilate said to them, 'You have a guard of soldiers; go, make it as secure as you can.' So they went and made the sepulcher secure by sealing the stone and setting a guard."

When whatever it was that happened that night had happened, the guardsmen came racing back from the tomb to say that it was empty. According to Matthew, the chief priests and the Pharisees bribed them to spread the rumor that the disciples had stolen the corpse under cover of darkness. Pocketing the cash, the soldiers did as they were told, and "this story," Matthew concludes, "has been spread among the Jews to this day."

If this story was a lie, then what was the truth? In the apocryphal Gospel of Peter, which was written a great many years after the event, it is wonderfully told how, far from being asleep, the soldiers were wide awake when all of a sudden the heavens opened and two figures descended in a great cloud of light. The soldiers immediately woke up everybody else who was there sharing the watch with them so that there was a whole crowd of eyewitnesses to vouch for what happened next. The stone at the mouth of the tomb rolled back by itself, and the two glowing figures went in. When they came out again, they were supporting between them a third figure who was followed by a miraculous cross. The heads of the original two "reached into heaven," the account says, "but of him that was led by them . . . it overpassed the heavens."

If Matthew, Mark, Luke, and John had wanted to concoct an account appropriate to the occasion, this is very much the kind of account they would probably have concocted, but instead of that they give virtually no account at all. In the canonical Gospels no story is told of how the body of Jesus

86

disappeared from the tomb. All that is said is that by the time the women got there, the stone had been rolled back and it was empty. What followed was chaos—dim figures flickering through the dawn, voices calling out, the sound of running feet. When the women got back to Jerusalem and gasped it all out to the disciples, Luke says that the disciples considered their words "an idle tale, and they did not believe them."

Who knows what the truth of it was? Maybe somebody really did steal the body at night while the guards were asleep, and Matthew is only attempting to explain it away. Maybe the apocryphal Gospel of Peter with its angels and miracles is closer to the facts than in our sophistication we are capable of imagining. Maybe it is the New Testament account with its picture of confusion and disbelief that rings most authentically— nobody ever knew exactly what happened because nobody was there to see it. Or maybe the tomb was empty because Jesus had never been put there in the first place but was just thrown into a common ditch with the two thieves who were crucified with him.

The earliest reference to the resurrection is Paul's, and he makes no mention of an empty tomb at all. But the fact of the matter is that in a way it hardly matters how the body of Jesus came to be missing because in the last analysis what convinced the people that he had risen from the dead was not the absence of his corpse but his living presence. And so it has been ever since.

Luke tells how, on that same third day, two of the disciples were on their way to a town called Emmaus a few miles out of Jerusalem when they were joined by a man they did not recognize. While they walked, he talked with them about the whole sad story of the Messiah and how he had died. When evening came and they reached their destination, the stranger indicated that he was going to keep on a while longer, but they persuaded him to stop and have supper with them. It was only when he blessed the bread and then broke it and gave it to them that they saw who he was.

They could hardly see the face of the stranger for the great sunflower of light that suddenly blossomed out behind it, but they saw enough to know that it was not a stranger who was standing there. The moment they knew who it was, he was gone.

On another occasion Thomas saw him too, of all the disciples the one who manages somehow to put his thumb on our hearts, the one from Missouri. He was known as the Twin, John says, and in some sense he is the twin of us all, this doubting Thomas. The disciples were hiding out in Jerusalem somewhere, scared out of their wits that the authorities who had taken care of Jesus would be arriving any moment to take care of them. They had bolted the door and were listening for the dreaded sound of footsteps on the stair when suddenly Jesus was among them. He stood there in their midst—always in the midst, this man turning up when they least expected him, maybe least wanted him—and told them to breathe in his breath, his holy breath and spirit, so that they could go out into the world again and perform his holy work. They all heard what he said with their ears and saw how he looked with their eyes except Thomas, who was not there. When he came back a while later, they told him what had happened. Thomas said, "Unless I see in his hands the print of the nails, and place my finger in the mark of the nails, and place my hand in his side, I will not believe." Thomas, our twin.

A week or so later Jesus appeared to them again, and this time Thomas *was* there. Jesus says, "Put your finger here, and see my hands; and put out your hand and place it in my side." To make it easier for Thomas, he undoes the top of his robe and holds his right arm up so that it will be out of the way. Thomas crouches down to touch the wound, and as he touches it, and only then, he says, "My Lord and my God!" and Jesus says, "Have you believed because you have seen me? Blessed are those who have not seen and yet believe."

It is the story of our lives, of course, as in some strange way the whole Bible is the story of our lives. Which of us hasn't known the innocence of Eden and tasted the sweetness of the forbidden tree? Which of us hasn't heard the angry thundering of the prophets in our own conscience and like Israel hoped against hope for a savior to deliver us from, if nothing else, ourselves? But Thomas's story is especially our story. Unless we see with our own eyes, we will not believe because we cannot believe, cannot believe fully anyway, cannot believe in a sense that affects the way we live our lives. Nearly two thousand Easters have taken place since Thomas's day, two thousand years of people proclaiming that the tomb was empty and the dead Christ alive among men to heal, to sustain, to transform. But it is not enough. If we are to believe in his resurrection in a way that really matters, we must somehow see him for ourselves. And wherever we have so believed, it is because in some sense we have seen him. Now as then, it is not his absence from the empty tomb that convinces men but the shadow at least of his presence in their empty lives.

In an apocryphal gospel, ascribed to Doubting Thomas himself, Jesus is depicted as saying, "Cleave a piece of wood, and I am there. Lift up the stone, and you will find me there." In other words, there is no place on earth too outlandish to find him in, no place on earth but where, in their outlandish yearning to see and thus believe, people have not believed that they have seen him. Blessed are they who have not seen as Thomas saw, and yet with the eyes of their yearning and their faith have seen enough.

"Have you believed because you have seen me?" he asked Thomas, and then, "Blessed are those who have not seen . . ." except ambiguously, obscurely, never sure whether what they have seen is the holiness at the heart of reality itself or only a shadow cast by their longing for holiness at the heart. John says that when Mary Magdalene saw him at the tomb that early dawn, she thought at first that he was the gardener. Maybe for the rest of her life she was never entirely sure.

In the Gospels, Jesus while still on earth foretells the Last Judgment. All the nations of the earth are drawn up before the Son of man, he says, and the Son of man will separate them from one another as a shepherd separates the sheep from the goats. Placing the souls of the righteous at his right hand, he says to them, "I was hungry and you gave me food, I was thirsty and you gave me drink, I was a stranger and you welcomed me, I was naked and you clothed me, I was sick and you visited me, I was in prison and you came to me," and when the righteous turn to him and ask when they can ever have had the opportunity to do such things for him, he answers them by saying, "as you did it to one of the least of these my brethren, you did it to me." And then the unrighteous, of course. "I was hungry and you gave me no food," he says—thirsty, a stranger, naked and sick and in prison—and to their shuddering question, *Lord, when?* he has a shuddering answer: "As you did it not to one the least of these, you did it not to me."

Thus for Jesus the only distinction among people that ultimately matters seems to be not whether they are churchgoers or non-churchgoers, Catholics or Protestants, Muslims or Jews, but do they or do they not love—love not in the sense of an emotion so much as in the sense of an act of the will, the loving act of willing another's good even, if need arise, at the expense of their own. "Hell is the suffering of being unable to love," said old Father Zossima or, as John puts it in his first epistle, "He who does not love abides in death."

"As you did it to one of the least of these my brethren, you did it to me." Just as Jesus appeared at his birth as a helpless child that the world was free to care for or destroy, so now he appears in his resurrection as the pauper, the prisoner, the stranger: appears in every form of human need that the world is free to serve or to ignore.

The risen Christ is Christ risen in his glory, but he is also Christ risen in the hearts of those who, although they have never touched the mark of the nails, have been themselves so touched by him that they believe anyway. However faded and threadbare, what they have seen of him is at least enough to get their bearings by.

Many would settle for the Resurrection as a metaphor for the unconquerable power of love in the world, for the undying spirit of Jesus which still has the power to touch and guide us as the spirit of Lincoln does, or Saint Francis, or Martin Luther King. Jesus triumphs as virtue triumphs, is alive as hope is alive, keeps returning to the world as springtime returns. Many a Christian sermon has been preached along such lines, and there are many outside the faith as well as inside it who would be willing to say "amen" to nothing more glorious than that. But not Paul.

It is no wonder that so many people deplore him as the one who defiled the pure stream of Jesus' teachings with unnecessary theological obscurities. It is no wonder that so many recoil from his arrogance, his ill-temper, his views on women, the divisive polemics that he fired off in those marvelous, punch-drunk letters with which he peppered the missionary churches of his time. But for better or worse, Paul spoke out what he believed to be the truth regardless of consequences, and for better or worse the truth as he spoke it has remained all these years the classic expression of Christian orthodoxy.

About the Resurrection Paul could hardly have been less obscure. "If Christ has not been raised, then our preaching is in vain and your faith is in vain," he wrote to the Corinthians. "If for this life only we have hoped in Christ, we are of all men most to be pitied. But in fact Christ has been raised from the dead, the first fruits of those who have fallen asleep. For as by man came death, by a man has come also the resurrection of the dead. For as in Adam all die, so also in Christ shall all be made alive."

For Paul the Resurrection was no metaphor; it was the power of God. And when he spoke of Jesus as raised from the dead, he meant Jesus alive and at large in the world not as some shimmering ideal of human goodness but as the very power of life itself. If the life that was in Jesus died on the cross; if the love that was in him came to an end when his heart stopped beating; if the truth that he spoke was no more if no less timeless than the great truths of any time; if all that he had in him to give to the world was a little glimmer of light to make bearable the inexorable approach of endless night—then all was despair.

To make sure that nobody missed the point, Paul spelled it out still further in his shattering bluntness. In speaking of the Resurrection of Christ as supremely real, it was supremely of Christ that he was speaking and of Christ's glory, but it was also of us and our glory. If Jesus has been raised from the dead, then all who have something of his life in them will be raised from the dead with him. If on the other hand, death was the end for Jesus, it will be the end for all of us whether we have his life in us or not; and if that is the case, then in the long run what does Jesus matter, what does anything matter? Paul makes the alternatives as sharp and simple as that and leaves no doubt which one he believes. "Lo! I tell you a mystery," he writes. "We shall all be changed in a moment, in the twinkling of an eye, at the last trumpet. . . . For this perishable nature must put on the imperishable, and this mortal nature must put on immortality. . . . [T]hanks be to God, who gives us the victory through our Lord Jesus Christ."

The face of Jesus is a face that belongs to us the way our past belongs to us. It is a face that we belong to as to the one face that has had more to do with the shaping of our present than any other. According to Paul, the face of Jesus is our own face finally, the face we will all come to look like a little when the Kingdom comes and we are truly ourselves at last, truly the brothers and sisters of one another and the children of God.

All those faces—they come drifting back at us like dreams: the solemn child in his mother's arms, the man scattering words and miracles like seed, the man eating for the last time with his friends, the Jew retching out his life from the cross of his pain.

What words do we face him with? Maybe the best are the words the Bible ends with: "Come, Lord Jesus." The unbeliever can say them along with the believer. Why not? If he exists somewhere beyond men's ancient longing for him, let him come then, with healing in his wings.

And what will he say to us as he comes? Let it be a little crazy because in terms of the world's grim sanity, he is a little crazy himself, and all who follow him are too. Let it be the words to the hymn that according to the apocryphal Acts of John he sang to his disciples at their last meal:

Glory be to thee, Father

Glory be to thee, Word. Glory be to thee, Grace. Amen

Glory be to thy glory. Amen

I would be saved, and I would save. Amen

I would be loosed, and I would loose. Amen

I would be wounded, and I would wound. Amen

I would be born, and I would bear. Amen

I would eat, and I would be eaten. Amen

I would hear, and I would be heard. Amen

Grace danceth. I would pipe. Dance ye all. Amen

I would mourn. Lament ye all. Amen

Whoso danceth not, knoweth not what cometh to pass. Amen

I would flee, and I would stay. Amen

I would adorn, and I would be adorned. Amen

I would be united, and I would unite. Amen

A house I have not, and I have houses. Amen

A lamp am I to thee that beholdest me. Amen

A mirror am I to thee that perceivest me. Amen

A door am I to thee that knockest at me. Amen

A way am I to thee a wayfarer. Amen

THUS, MY BELOVED,

HAVING DANCED WITH US,

THE LORD WENT FORTH.

ABOUT PARACLETE PRESS

Who We Are

Paraclete Press is an ecumenical publisher of books on Christian spirituality for people of all denominations and backgrounds.

We publish books that represent the wide spectrum of Christian belief and practice—from Catholic to Evangelical to liturgical to Orthodox.

We market our books primarily through booksellers; we are what is called a "trade" publisher, which means that we like it best when readers buy our books from booksellers, our partners in successfully reaching as wide an audience as possible.

We are uniquely positioned in the marketplace without connection to large corporation or conglomerate and with informal relationships to many branches and denominations of faith, rather than a formal relationship to any single one. We focus on publishing a diversity of thoughts and perspectives—the fruit of our diversity as a company.

What We Are Doing

Paraclete Press is publishing books that show the diversity and depth of what it means to be Christian. We publish books that reflect the Christian experience across many cultures, time periods, and houses of worship.

We publish books about spiritual practice, history, ideas, customs and rituals, and books that nourish the vibrant life of the church.

We have several different series of books within Paraclete Press, including the bestselling Living Library series of modernized classic texts, A Voice from the Monastery—giving voice to men and women monastics on what it means to live a spiritual life today, and Many Mansions—exploring the riches of the world's religious traditions and discovering how other faiths inform Christian thought and practice.

Learn more about us at our website: www.paracletepress.com, or call us toll-free at 1-800-451-5006.

Also Available from Paraclete Press

The Wet Engine
ISDN: 1-55725-405-2
170 pages
$17.95, Hardcover

The heart: It is known as the seat of the soul, the powerhouse of the body, the essence of spirituality. No other bodily organ has so captured the imagination of human beings since the beginning of time. The profoundly moving rumination in *The Wet Engine* will change how you feel and think about the mysterious, fragile, human heart.

"Brian Doyle's spirit is catching: it will catch you up,
and soon you will have caught on to everything he feels and ruminates over
and marvels at, and you will comprehend what poetry is and does.
And you will know from the throb of *The Wet Engine*,
this unique and beautiful book written in celestial prose,
that Brian Doyle is as glorious a poet as he is a father; and vice versa."
—Cynthia Ozick

The Coming of Christ
Gloriæ Dei Cantores Schola
Conducted by Mary Berry
CD, ISDN:1-55725-310-2 , $16.95

Rendered in the lush and sacred sounds of Gregorian chant, *The Coming of Christ* celebrates the seasons of Advent, Christmas, and Epiphany. The music expresses the intense human longing for the birth of Christ and the joy of the angel's message.

"Gramophone's own Mary Berry conducts with unassailable authority.
The singers create an atmosphere that is retained impressively throughout."
—Gramophone

"Splendid singing. . . .
Gloriae Dei Cantores Schola specialize in the daily singing of Gregorian chant
and their familiarity with its various repertoires is very much in evidence in
this wide-ranging anthology."
—International Record Review

Available from most booksellers or through Paraclete Press
www.paracletepress.com
1-800-451-5006
Try your local bookstore first.